MW01181980

raising a pure
generation
parent's guide

With Transforming Your Family Personal Devotional

JULIE HIRAMINE
with the Generations of Virtue Team

GENERATIONS
OF VIRTUE

www.generationsofvirtue.org

Raising a Pure Generation: Parent's Guide
Copyright © 2012 by Generations of Virtue

Published by: Generations of Virtue
                    P.O. Box 1353
                    Monument, CO 80132
                    www.generationsofvirtue.org

All rights reserved. No part of this publication may be reproduced, stored in a
retrieval system, or transmitted in any form or by any means electronic, mechanical,
digital, photocopy, recording, or any other except for brief quotations in printed
reviews without the prior written permission of the publisher.

Unless otherwise noted, scripture quotations are taken from the New International
Version of the Bible. Copyright © 1973, 1978, 1984, International Bible Society.

contents

introduction

Dear Parent,

Thank you so much for joining us for the *Raising a Pure Generation* curriculum. I trust that you are a parent, like so many others, who desires to see your children walk in purity before the Lord. What this means - in the midst of a world whose value system is in opposition to our own - is nothing short of raising a generation to make radically different choices than their peers and the culture around them.

If you are like other parents I know, your desire is to see your children make wise choices about things like friends, media, and relationships. You long to see your children follow the Lord with their hearts, minds, and bodies. It's not going to be a simple task, but you as the parent are the most influential element in this equation. We cannot accomplish this without God's help and His direction. All around the world, I see God raising up a generation to stand pure against the tide of culture.

Yours is a mission directed by God Almighty, and I want to encourage you as you endeavor to raise this pure generation. Trust the Lord to equip you in this battle. I am convinced that as you intercede, train and pray for your children regarding their purity, the Lord will meet you and provide the wisdom and strength you need to do this. May the Lord bless you and pour out His spirit on you as you start this journey.

For the Kingdom,
Julie Hiramine

session one:
family connectedness

[
"You don't choose your family. They are God's gift
to you, as you are to them."
~Desmond Tutu
]

family connectedness

Come On In! In a world that doesn't leave us much room for being connected as a family, parents have to be very intentional about spending time together, mentoring their kids, and doing things to build relationship. This session focuses on giving parents the 4 keys to helping their kids avoid high-risk behavior. Join us as we look at ways to lay a godly foundation for your family.

There are 4 keys parents can practice to help their kids avoid high risk behavior:

> 1. Family connectedness
>> • Ideas to connect: dinner as a family, family devotions

> 2. Express Clear Expectations
>> • Kids need to hear "no" to be able to say it themselves

"Rules without relationship lead to rebellion, while relationship without rules leads to confusion."
—Josh McDowell

Girls are 250% more likely to engage in sexual behavior if their fathers are not involved with them on a predictable basis.[1]

NOTES

_____

_____

_____

_____

_____

_____

_____

_____

_____

_____

_____

1. Society for Research in Child Development, "Fathers Respond To Teens' Risky Sexual Behavior With Increased Supervision". ScienceDaily, (2009, May 21). http://www.sciencedaily.com/releases/2009/05/090515083700.htm.

3. Positive Input
   • Mom and Dad are the number one influence

4. A father's involvement
   • Dad, you are important! If kids don't get attention from Dad, they will look for it somewhere else.

The following resource recommendations are taken from *Against the Tide,* a purity curriculum for parents to go through with their children.

 recommended resources

Birth – 8 years
My Big Book of 5 Minute Devotions by Pamela Kennedy and Douglas Kennedy
His Little Princess by Sheri Rose Shepherd
His Mighty Warrior by Sheri Rose Shepherd

8-12 years
Secret Keeper Girl Kit 2 by Dannah Gresh
Boyhood and Beyond by Bob Schultz

Teens
Developing Godly Character by Vinnie Carafano
Teknon and the Champion Warriors by Brent Sapp (ages 11-16)

Parents
Loving Our Kids on Purpose by Danny Silk
Age of Opportunity by Paul David Tripp

 **Need some inspiration?**
Check out www.generationsfvirtue.org for resources and easy ways to connect together!

 tech tip

Use the technology available to you to connect with your kids. Some ideas:

+ If your kids have their own cell phones, text them encouraging messages, or just let them know you are praying for them.

+ If you have to travel, Skype with your kids. Jump on the computer to get some face-to-face time. Ask them about what they did that day, how they are feeling, etc. Tell them about your day. Pray for them over Skype.

+ Email – Send your kids letters through email. Even if you have a busy schedule, email allows you to write a quick note whenever you have a chance.

+ If your kids are on Facebook, write them an encouraging message on their walls, mention them in a post, or send them a message.

The point here is you want to engage your kids in their environment. They are constantly surrounded by media, messages, and devices – why not create some positive messages they can look forward to receiving? Use the convenience of technology to your advantage.

 ways to connect

+ Have to dash out to the grocery store? Take a kid with you. Every once in a while it's good to give your kids one-on-one time where they can feel free to talk to you and be themselves.

+ Affirm each child once every day this week. As you see them doing good things, tell them about it! Also, be sure to affirm who they are, and not only what they do.

 weekly challenge

Everyday this week, play the game "A Rose, a Thorn and Spaghetti". This fun and easy game is perfect for the whole family, and a great way to connect together! (It makes a great dinner time game.) Here are the rules: Have your family sit together in a circle and ask each person to share their "rose, thorn, and spaghetti" for the day:

Rose: Something fantastic or delightful that happened today (this teaches thankfulness, no matter how discouraging our day is; looking for the positive)

Thorn: Something challenging or adverse that happened today

Spaghetti: Something silly or funny that happened today

Allow each person to share. You'll be surprised at the laughs and insight you'll get as you give each child the opportunity to share - whether they are 2 or 17! While you're together as a family, why not take a moment to pray together? Ask your kids if they have any prayer requests and take time to come together before the throne of God. These special times are key in building family connectedness.

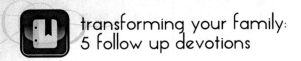

transforming your family: 5 follow up devotions

Day 1: Read Deuteronomy 6: 4-9. Pray about the example you are showing your kids. Do they see from your actions, your speech, your instructions, that the Lord is your God?

+ Wait upon the Lord and ask Him if there are any actions toward one of your children that He would want you to change. Ask Him to transform that today.
+ Is there something you have said or a pattern of speaking to your kids that God needs to change? Bring this area before Him and submit it to Him.
+ Are you intentionally instructing your kids in the ways of the Lord? Ask God to give you one idea that you can do this week with your family.

Day 2: Read Ephesians 4:1-3. Are there any areas of tension between you and members of your family that is making it difficult to connect? Lift these areas up before the Lord and ask Him to work out these problems. As you wait on the Lord, seek Him for His divine answers to the difficulty you face today.

Day 3: Read 1 John 2:3-6. Pray specifically about the example of obedience you give your kids. Do they see you seeking God's direction on a daily basis? Do they see you follow His direction? Ask God to show you one area He wants you to examine where He wants growth.

Day 4: Read Romans 7:21-25. Is there anything you see yourself doing that you don't want to pass on to your kids? Pray specifically about this issue. Ask God to sever the generational sin that gets passed down to the 3rd and 4th generation (Numbers 14:18). Ask the Lord to change the next generation and commit them to Him.

> • Is there anything negative that was passed from your parents to you that you want to be cut off before the next generation inherits it?

Day 5: Read Ephesians 5:15-16. Time with your family is short. Pray about ways you can make the most of the time you are given with your children. What areas of your daily life could you open up and allow your family into? Are there any things you do regularly that you can invite a kid or two to join you on?

session two:
parents: guardians of purity

["The ultimate test of a moral society is the kind of
world that it leaves to its children."
~Dietrich Bonhoeffer]

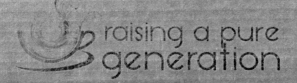

raising a pure
generation

parents: guardians of purity

Come On In! If our kids are going to be able to stand against the tide of impurity in our culture, we as parents must learn to be the ultimate protectors of their purity. This session is foundational in helping you understand what it means to be your children's guardians, and how to build an impenetrable wall to protect against the forces of darkness that try to come against our children. As you participate in this session, ask yourself: how do I want my kids to be on their wedding day? How will they get there?

Hollywood's love story versus God's love story

4 things parents have to be to guard their children's purity

1. Intentional

2. Purposeful

"Your virtues train your attitudes, attitudes dictate your choices, choices decide your behavior, and your behavior determines your destiny. The way that this whole process begins is by giving your virtues authority over your thoughts. If your virtues do not govern what you allow yourself to think about, this process of reaching your destiny will be sabotaged. Trying to behave inside your virtues, without taking control of what movie is being shown in the theater room of your heart, simply won't work. Everything in life begins with a thought, an image that is projected on the movie screen of your mind."[1]

1. Vallotton, Kris and Jason Vallotton, *Moral Revolution: The naked truth about sexual purity.* Destiny Image Publishers: 2010.

3. Protecting
- Nehemiah builds the wall (book of Nehemiah)

- Proverbs 4:23

4. Persevering
- Isaiah 55:11 – God's word does not return void

recommended resources

Parents

Moral Revolution: The naked truth about sexual purity
   by Kris Vallotton and Jason Vallotton
Boy's Passage, Man's Journey by Brian Molitor
Girl's Passage, Father's Duty by Brian Molitor

Check out www.generationsfvirtue.org
for these resources and more!

tech tip

Evaluate your own use of technology. As a guardian
of your children's purity, are you using technology
to access things you would never want your child
to? Take an honest look at the movies you watch,
songs you listen to, etc. Is there anywhere in your use
of technology where you've let in a little bit of evil?
Where you've slackened your grip on your job as
guardian of your home? Our guarding needs to start
with ourselves – so that we will be able to help our
children with the same standards.

NOTES

_____
_____
_____
_____
_____
_____
_____
_____
_____
_____
_____
_____
_____
_____
_____
_____
_____
_____
_____
_____
_____
_____

 ways to connect

Read the story of Adam and Eve in Genesis 3 with your kids. Explain to them the concept of knowledge versus experience. If your kids are younger, give them another word picture that is a little more relatable to their situations. (IE: "It's like that time I told you not to touch the pan on the stove. You listened to me and didn't touch it – so you chose knowledge. But if you hadn't listened and touched it, you would have learned by experience that pans on the stove are hot and can burn you.")

 weekly challenge

As behavior issues pop up this week, take a minute to go further with your kids. Instead of just correcting the immediate issue, consider if there are things that God is nudging at that may be a bit deeper, things that may be a heart motive or intention that is not right. For instance, if your child has the habit of telling "little white lies", begin to look at the deeper root. Why are they doing this? What is their motive? Ask God to give you wisdom for each specific situation.

transforming your family:
5 follow up devotions

The following devotions will focus on the first half of the book of Nehemiah. As you study the scripture, relate the walls to the protection around your child's purity. Look at these next five days as a concentrated effort to see where the walls around your family's purity may be in disrepair and need rebuilding. Where has the enemy been able to attack you as a family – specifically in the area of purity - because of this disrepair?

Day 1: Read Nehemiah chapters 1 and 2:1-8. Nehemiah started the process of rebuilding the walls by prayer, fasting, and repenting. Begin these five days by fasting and praying. Repent of places of impurity in your own heart (whether it be past or present). Repent on behalf of your children and your spouse as Nehemiah repented on behalf of Israel.

- Instead of just fasting food, ask God if there is a specific kind of media He wants you to fast from and take the time you would be spending with that book, TV show, movie, website, etc. to spend time with the Lord.
- Wait on the Lord to bring an area to your mind and then spend time repenting. The Lord Himself will search out our hearts of areas that need to be surrendered to Him; even if these areas are from years past. (Psalm 19:12)

Day2: Read Nehemiah 2:9-20 and chapter 3. Today, assess the walls in your family. What damage has the enemy been able to do because of the disrepair? Inspect the damage and pray about how to rebuild your walls. As the Lord leads and as it is appropriate, talk to your family about the damage.

- For instance, are there movies you've watched recently that had a negative message that has affected your children negatively? What about songs, video games, activities, etc.?
- As the first line of defense between the enemy and your children, are there openings in your life that are allowing bad influences to come in? Ask the Lord right now what these openings are and how to repair them.

Day 3: Read Nehemiah chapter 4. What influences are hindering your work of rebuilding the wall? Is it the culture? Friends or friend's families? Identify these influences and pray about them. Ask the Lord to protect you and your family from any nay-sayers who would have you believe it's not possible to stand for purity in our culture.

- Ask God to give you one new idea on how to be in the world but not of it (John 17:15-16 and Romans 12:2)
- Wait on God; the idea that is from Him will be like a light turning on. It will be an "aha" moment or something like "wow, I never thought of it like this before!"
- Think about the appetites you create in your children. Are you allowing "tastes" of things that are going to become unhealthy appetites in the future?

Day 4: Read Nehemiah chapter 5. This chapter talks about the oppression of the poor by the officials and nobles. Apply this chapter to the members of your family. Is anyone doing something that is hindering a brother or sister in his or her walk for purity? Is there anything you are doing as a parent that is frustrating your kids, making it difficult for them to obey God's direction about purity? Ask the Lord to show you areas where oppression may be going on in your family.

• Ask God to shine His light on relational dynamics especially between siblings. Remember, you are not just focusing on purity of body. Are there any relational dynamics that do not reflect purity of heart and mind? (IE: thoughts our kids think about one another that are just not very nice!) Ask God to give you strategies to tackle this.

Day 5: Read Nehemiah chapter 6. In this chapter, Nehemiah rightly antici-
pates and avoids a conspiracy against himself. Today, ask the Lord to
show you any plots from the enemy targeted at you, specifically to dis-
tract you from the work of building walls around your family. Where
is the enemy trying to intimidate you or the members of your family?
Pray for freedom from fear and oppression from the enemy.

session three:
building a pure foundation

["Children are not casual guests in our home.
They have been loaned to us temporarily
for the purpose of loving them and instilling a
foundation of values on which their future
lives will be built.."
~Dr. James Dobson]

session 3

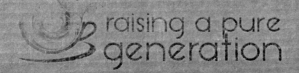

raising a pure
generation

building a pure foundation

Come On In! You as parents are the gatekeepers of your home. It is up to you to determine how wide or how narrow the gate of influence is left open to allow the culture in. Sometimes it can be difficult to determine which influences will be helpful or harmful to your children in the long run. This session focuses on the tools that you as parents need in order to "guard the gate".

Birth – 8 years

What are we putting into the foundations of our kids' lives?

Don't let movies and video games be babysitters

Babysitters

Honoring boundaries

Helping with chores

> "Most often, sexual abusers know the child they abuse but are not relatives. In fact, about 60% of perpetrators are non-relative acquaintances, such as a friend of the family, babysitter, or neighbor. About 30% of those who sexually abuse children are relatives of the child, such as fathers, uncles, or cousins."[1]

NOTES

_____

_____

_____

_____

_____

_____

_____

1. Julia Whealin, Ph.D. (2007-05-22). "Child Sexual Abuse". National Center for Post Traumatic Stress Disorder, US Department of Veterans Affairs.

Tweens 8-12 years
Manners

• Boys especially need to learn how to honor and respect women

Conscience needs to stay pure and able to be touched by God

Chores

11 - 12 is a special time of opportunity

> *"Trust everyone – verify everything"*
> —Ronald Reagan

Teens

Wake up and smell the coffee
  - Examining intents and motives

Keep things out in the open

Lie is we have to be the perfect family

We don't need to be perfect – but willing to bend our knees at the foot of the cross

recommended resources

Birth – 8 years
The Swimsuit Lesson by Jon Holsten
Everyday Graces by Karen Santorum

8-12 years
Created for Work by Bob Schultz
My Best Friend, Jesus by Dannah Gresh

Teens
A Young Woman's Guide to Making Right Choices by Elizabeth George
A Young Man's Guide to Making Right Choices by Jim George

Parents
The Danger of Raising Nice Kids by Timothy Smith

tech tip

Keeping tech devices out in public areas is an easy way to keep your kids away from questionable material. Position things like computers and video game consoles in high traffic areas where people will be filtering through on a predictable basis. As much as possible, have the screens facing out, where a passerby will be able to see what's going on. This will enable you to take quick looks at the screen and deter your kids from intentionally going anywhere questionable on these devices. Another good idea is to have device curfews. At night, you can have all the cell phones, laptops, mp3 players, etc. charge in your room, making them inaccessible to youngsters who should be sleeping. If you have an immovable desktop, there are settings you can implement so certain users are only allowed on at certain times. The point is you want to make these devices unavailable to your children during times when they are more likely to get into trouble (either intentionally or unintentionally).

 ways to connect

The next time your son or daughter expresses an interest in a video game, movie, or album, sit through watching or listening to it with him or her. Play the video game, watch the movie, listen to the whole album (if it passes your media standards test, of course). This will give you an opportunity to engage your son or daughter in something that is of interest to him or her. It will create an avenue for you to discuss things like the content of the game, movie, or song.

 weekly challenge

This week, implement a "Manners Week"[2] – a week-long concentrated effort to practice good manners. At the beginning of the week, go over with your family the basic manners you want to practice this week. It may be saying things like "please pass the butter" at the dinner table instead of "hey – gimme the butter!", or it could involve deeper issues like cleaning up after yourself instead of expecting someone else to. Mom and Dad need to be diligent to practice good manners as well! At the end of the week, debrief with one another and evaluate how the week went. What did you learn? What do you need to keep working on?

2. We originally got the idea of "Manners Week" from Dennis and Barbara Rainey, who talk about it on their radio program, FamilyLife Today.

transforming your family:
5 follow up devotions

Day 1: Read Jeremiah 29:11-13 and Isaiah 42:6. Pray today about God's calling for each of your children. Ask Him to show you and your children very clearly what His specific calling is for each one of them as they grow up.

Day 2: Read Hebrews 11:8-11 and think about all Abraham and Sarah did in faith – not knowing why or what would come of it. Ask the Lord what He wants to put in the foundations of your children's lives. Since only He knows what they will be doing in the future, He knows what is the best preparation for that future.

- Think specifically about chores as you are praying. Are there any chores, like the laundry, that you could have your kids take responsibility for?

Day 3: Read Romans 2: 6-8. Pray specifically about your children's areas of disobedience. Lift these issues up to the Lord and ask Him to reconcile them to Him. As you are praying for your children, lift up your own issues of disobedience. Are there areas you are seeing where your example of disobedience is hindering your children from making the right choices?

Day 4: Read 2 Timothy 3:16, John 6:63, Psalm 119:125 and 119:130. Ask the Lord today to give you and your children an inextinguishable love for God's Word. Ask Him to help you memorize it, read it daily personally and as a family, and understand it. Ask Him to give you a verse you can write down and memorize today.

Day 5: Make a list of strengths for each child. Now make a list of areas that are weaknesses they need to work through. Pray that God would show you the intents and motives of their hearts.

- Can you identify a "romantic" in your family? How can you help this child keep love asleep while finding an appropriate outlet for those feelings?
- Now think about your whole family – do you have a media junkie? Is the TV news on all the time at your home? Do you need to make some adjustments? What kind of time limits do you institute in your home with media?

session four:
developing purity muscles

["It is easier to build strong children
than to repair broken men."
~Frederick Douglas]

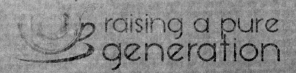
raising a pure
generation

developing purity muscles

Come On In! If our kids are going to have strong values when it comes to purity, then we must begin building those muscles now, not wait until they are 15 or 16 and expect them to succeed! Think of it like this: You would never expect your teen to finish a marathon if she can barely run a mile. You would never expect your child to ace a chemistry exam if he has never taken the class. It is the same when it comes to their purity! They need to be trained and prepared so that they can stand strong for purity and holiness in today's dark world.

Helping their body image

Girls

+ Modesty

Boys

+ Bouncing eyes and pornography

The average age of first exposure to pornography is 11[1]

1. Family Safe Media http://www.familysafemedia.com/pornography_statistics.html

"Be angry and do not
sin; do not let the
sun go down on
your anger."
—Ephesians 4:26 ESV

NOTES

_____

_____

_____

_____

_____

_____

_____

_____

_____

_____

_____

_____

_____

What are they taking in?

Siblings

Talking to kids about the birds and the bees

Give kids vision for the things God has called
them to

2. The idea of using your family relationships as training for marriage originally
came from Eric and Leslie Ludy, who expand upon the concept in their book,
Teaching True Love to a Sex-at-Thirteen Generation. Thomas Nelson: 2005.

recommended resources

Birth – 8 years
His Little Princess by Sheri Rose Shepherd
His Mighty Warrior by Sheri Rose Shepherd

8-12 years
Secret Keeper Girl by Dannah Gresh
Everyday Battles by Bob Schultz
The Popularity Myth: Equip your daughter to embrace true friendship CD by
   Julie Hiramine

Teens
How to Ruin Your Life by 40 by Steve Farrar
Secret Keeper by Dannah Gresh

Parents
Preparing Your Son for Every Man's Battle by Stephen Arterburn and
   Fred Stoeker
Six Ways to Keep the "Little" in Your Girl by Dannah Gresh

tech tip

Limiting the time your kids are allowed to do things like play video games or watch television will help them develop self-control in the area of technology. Kids need to learn that they can't spend all their time doing something that doesn't produce any fruit. It's better to use technology as a way to take a break every once in a while rather than let it consume our kids' time. The key to setting time limits, though, is to enforce them. Remember: you are the parent. You determine how long and how frequently it is appropriate to use something, then help your kids abide by these boundaries.

 ways to connect

As your kids leave for school, a lesson, or go to a friend's house, pray for them. Ask them if they want you to pray specifically about anything in particular. Is there anything they are nervous about? What do they hope to get out of the time? Pray for your kids out loud, in their presence.

 weekly challenge

This week, set aside a time (or two) to worship together as a family. Even if you don't play any instruments, you can find worship lyrics online and sing. It doesn't have to be a super ceremonious event that takes planning and lots of time to prepare. Your worship time can be as simple as finding some song lyrics or recorded worship music, gathering the family together, singing, and then closing your time in prayer. You can also sing a worship song when you sit down to dinner and pray for the meal. If you are a musical family, invite members to play their instruments. The point is this is your time as a family to gather together and worship God for who He is – not how well you can play or sing!

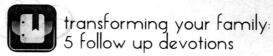
transforming your family:
5 follow up devotions

Day 1: Read 2 Chronicles 20:15-24. Worship is a powerful tool we can use to change our situations. Spend some time worshipping the Lord before you start praying today.
- After you are done worshipping, pray about ways you can serve together as a family.

Day 2: Read Ephesians 6:10-18. Developing muscles is a process that requires repetition and discipline. Just like purity, it's a practice that you can't just stop and take a break from. Ask the Lord for perseverance and endurance for this battle for your family's purity. Ask God what specific battle He wants you to put on the armor of God for and fight today.

Day 3: Read Matthew 6:33. Evaluate your personal relationship with Christ today. Before you can truly disciple your children in having a deep, intentional relationship with Christ, you must have one yourself. How do you model this love relationship with God to your kids? What areas of this relationship is He asking you to work on?

Day 4: Read Matthew 5:22-24. Pray about your kids' relationships with one another (sibling relationships). If you only have one child, pray about your child's relationships with peers, cousins, or close friends. Do you notice points of contention that need to be worked through? Ask the Lord to show you how to help your kids learn how to use these relationships to gain practice in self-sacrifice.

- Think about how your kids resolve conflict. Help them see the patterns they develop now will carry into their future relationships.

Day 5: Read 1 Corinthians 15:33 and pray about the influences in your children's lives. Think about the friends with whom they are keeping company, then think about the media with which they are keeping company. Ask the Lord if you need to sever any ties with this company.

session five:

media discernment

["In Beverly Hills, they don't throw their
garbage away, they make it into television shows."
~Woody Allen]

session 5

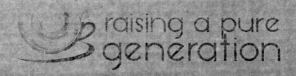
raising a pure
generation

media discernment

Come On In! While many parents want to see their children successfully navigate the waves of culture, few parents realize that that training needs to begin at a young age. There will be times at every stage of your child's development that will provide opportunities for you to sow seeds of purity and holiness, especially when it comes to media discernment. Helping your kids look at media from the perspective of what is harmful versus what is of value is a process, and that can begin today.

Setting the standard for romance and relationships
Dating and physical standards

Discerning the media's message
What are they trying to sell you?

_____

_____

_____

_____

_____

_____

_____

_____

_____

_____

_____

_____

_____

_____

_____

_____

_____

_____

Guarding against pornography
How can we protect our kids?

Filtering and accountability software
Good rule: If it goes online, it needs to be monitored

1. The concept of Digital Natives and Digital Immigrants mentioned in the video is taken from "Digital Natives, Digital Immigrants" by Marc Prensky. *On the Horizon* (MCB University Press, Vol. 9 No. 5, October 2001)

recommended resources

Birth to 8 years
The Princess and the Kiss by Jennie Bishop
The Squire and the Scroll by Jennie Bishop
This Is No Fairy Tale by Dale Tolmasoff

8-12 years
Life Lessons from Princess and the Kiss by Jennie Bishop and Susan Henson
Life Lessons from Squire and the Scroll by Jennie Bishop and Susan Henson

Teens
Connecting with God by Ron Luce
A Young Man's Guide to Making Right Choices by Jim George
Hero: Becoming the man she desires by Fred and Jasen Stoeker
His Princess: Girl talk with God by Sheri Rose Shepherd

For Parents
The Danger of Raising Nice Kids by Timothy Smith
Preparing Your Son for Every Man's Battle by Stephen Arterburn and Fred Stoeker
Preparing Your Daughter for Every Woman's Battle by Shannon Ethridge
Information Technology 101 CD By Julie Hiramine

 tech tip

In today's society, filtering software is no longer just a good idea, but an essential. Consider that "Pornography has a larger revenue than Microsoft, Google, Amazon, eBay, Yahoo, Apple and Netflix combined."[2] Unfortunately, stumbling onto a pornographic site is nearly unavoidable. So how do we protect our kids online? How do we monitor their internet usage to help keep them on the right track? Enter: filtering and accountability software. These tools help you block inappropriate websites, monitor what is being done online and how much time is spent. For our favorites, visit www.generationsofvirtue.org today!

 ways to connect

Imagine it: your kids, completely unintentionally, stumble upon something inappropriate online or on the TV. They run in to you and say, "I saw something ummmm.....ummmmm.....bad!" Well, as we both know, "bad" can mean a lot of things. To help your kids feel more comfortable should they ever have to tell you when they see something, this week, create a code word for these types of pornographic or inappropriate imagery. It could be something simple like, "Code Blue". Whatever it is, creating comfortable terms can help with openness and honesty when it comes to these sensitive issues - especially when our kids are with friends.

2. Taken from http://internet-filter-review.toptenreviews.com/internet-pornography-statistics.html

 weekly challenge

This week, sit down with your spouse and create a media contract both for you as adults and for your family. (Take a look at the Technology Tools page on www.generationsofvirtue.org for a full list of tips and ideas to consider as you make your media contract.) Include things like:

- We commit to honoring God with our media choices, so anything that includes obscenity or sexual content, we will skip (or not watch).
- We will turn in any and all electronics before bed time
- We will not watch movies with R or PG-13 ratings that have unwholesome content
- We will shut off the commercials during sports games
- We will put necessary safeguards in place on devices that can access the internet

.... you get the idea!

Our job as parents is to be an example of someone who is pursuing holiness - even in our media choices. Take this opportunity as a couple to adjust any media standards that need overhauling. We cannot expect our children to be pure if we are not! Print out your media contract and place it in prominent areas around your home. This way, everyone will know and remember the expectations. Creating this contract may mean that you will need to get rid of some of the movies you currently have in your home, and that's okay! If your kids ask you why, be sure to explain to them that you as a family are reaching for a high media standard.

For more resources and encouragement, including Julie's blog, visit us online at www.generationsofvirtue.org!

transforming your family: 5 follow up devotions

Day 1: Psalm 101:3a says "I will refuse to look at anything vile or vulgar." (NLT) When it comes to media, are you looking at or listening to anything vile or vulgar? Are your children? How do you think "vile" media affects your thinking? What about for your children?

Day 2: Read 2 Timothy 4:3-4. Someone once said, "Never confuse the will of the majority with the will of God." With media and our children, oftentimes the voice of Hollywood is seen as the voice of everyone. Now, you as an adult know that is not true, but do your children? Ask the Lord to show you how to teach your kids to believe the Word of God instead of the word of the majority.

Day 3: Douglas Gresham, stepson of the renowned C.S. Lewis, once said, "*In today's world, we look at our presidents, our princes... as our leaders, but they're not. They're merely our rulers. The leaders are the people who change the minds and stimulate the imaginations of the public...That means movie makers, the people who make TV shows, the entertainment people in the business.*" Do you find this statement to be true? Why or why not? If it is true, who is currently the greater influence on your child: the media or you? Ask the Lord to help you influence your children the way He wants you to.

Day 4: Many, many youth around the world have confided to us that they have seen their mother or father viewing pornography. Now, these are not non-Christian families. These are conservative parents and teens who are witnessing firsthand what the porn industry is doing to families.

- In Galatians 5:9, the Word says "A little yeast spreads through the whole batch of dough." (God's Word Translation) Our sin does not merely confine itself to one area of our lives, it permeates every thing, the very nature of our being. With this understanding, is there anything in your home, on your computer, or in your heart that needs to come into the light? Pray for the Lord to bring things into the light – both in yourself and in your children.

Day 5: Read Colossians 1:16. As Christians, we believe that God created *everything* and that He created *everything* to serve His purposes. Now, let's apply that truth to media and technology. Though sometimes it can be tempting to look at it all like garbage, how do we see it from God's perspective? What are some ways that your family can use the media, technology and resources at your fingertips to serve the Kingdom of God?

session six:

the birds and the bees

["Each day of our lives we make deposits
in the memory banks of our children."
~Charles R. Swindoll]

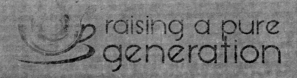

raising a pure
generation

the birds and the bees

Come On In! Nothing gets parents in a cold sweat faster than bringing up "the talk". But whether your kids are 2 or 20, this subject has to be broached at some point. There are natural stages for sharing with your children about this sensitive issue with age-appropriate information. Once you are armed with the right resources and an understanding of what to actually say, you'll be ready! Remember: You as parents are the experts when it comes to your kids. By being open and willing to share with your child about sex, you are giving them God's perfect design from the very beginning, and that is an incredible gift.

The first message is the most important
Giving our kids the perspective of God's awesome plan

What to discuss when our kids are little
Using the proper body terms

"Adolescents whose parents talk with them about standards of sexual behavior are more likely to be abstinent. Youths whose parents talked to them about what is right and wrong in sexual behavior were significantly more likely to be abstinent than peers whose parents did not."[1]

How to approach this in the tween years
Especially regarding development

"The Talk" and our own past
Is there anything stopping you from sharing with your kids?

1. Cheryl B. Aspy et al., "Parental Communication and Youth Sexual Behavior" *Journal of Adolescence*, No. 30 (2007): 449-466.

Innocence is not ignorance[2]

Jesus says the truth will set us free (John 8:32). If we – loving moms and dads – are honest with our kids about the facts of life, it will set them free from the influences of the culture trying to lie to them about issues of sexuality.

2. The inspiration for this phrase came from Dennis and Barbara Rainey's radio series entitled *"Beyond Abstinence"*. FamilyLife Today, 1997.
3. The statistic mentioned in the video about 1 in 3 girls having been molested by age 18 is taken from "Child Safe Tips" http://childsafetips.abouttips.com/child-molestation-statistics.

 recommended resources

Birth-8 years
The Swimsuit Lesson by Jon Holsten
The Wonderful Way Babies Are Made by Larry Christenson
The Miracle of Creation Series by Susan Horner

8-12 years
Beautifully Made! Series edited by Julie Hiramine
Lintball Leo's Not-So-Stupid Questions about Your Body by Dr. Walt Larimore
Passport 2 Purity by Dennis and Barbara Rainey
What Is God's Design for My Body? By Susan Horner

Teens
What's the Big Deal? by Stan and Brenna Jones
The Pathway of Purity that Leads to Purpose CD by Julie Hiramine
Nobody Told Me by Pam Stenzel and Melissa Nesdahl
What Are You Waiting For? by Dannah Gresh

Parents
Moral Revolution: The naked truth about sexual purity by Kris Vallotton and
   Jason Vallotton
Hooked by Dr. Joe S. McIhaney and Dr. Freda McKissic Bush
Teaching True Love to a Sex-At-13 Generation by Eric and Leslie Ludy
When Good Kids Make Bad Choices by Elise Fitzpatrick and Jim Newheiser

You may want to check out the *Against the Tide* purity curriculum from Generations of Virtue. It is an age-by-age guide to the key resources for talking with your kids about sex and purity from preschool through 8th grade. Also, feel free to check out www.generationsofvirtue.org for recommendations for your family on these key topics.

 tech tip

These days, photos and videos can be uploaded to the internet from anywhere in the world in the blink of an eye. Those photos and videos, even if deleted, remain in the world wide web's databases permanently. Did you catch that? Even if you delete or remove a photo/video from the internet, it is there, for any "techie" to access…forever. We need to teach our kids to guard what they upload to the internet. Are their pictures and videos completely appropriate?

Now, it's not just the pictures and videos that they themselves are uploading. ANYONE can take a snapshot and upload that video or picture of you or for you. So it becomes an issue of being above board in our actions all the time, because you never know when a camera, cell phone or iPod is watching.

 ways to connect

This week, ask your child, "What are 3 things you want in your future husband/wife someday?" Discuss what their hopes and dreams are for their future marriage. Is there anything they can be doing to prepare for their future right now? Consider the old saying, "In order to marry the right person, you need to be the right person."

 weekly challenge

This week, take some time with your spouse to discuss each child's sex education and purity training. Outline which resources you want to use with each child, what they are ready to hear, etc. Develop an outline for when you are going to talk to each child about things like:
- Body parts
- Sex
- Dating and relationships
- "The Swimsuit Lesson"
…. And whatever else you want to address!

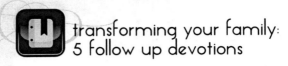

transforming your family:
5 follow up devotions

Day 1: Sometimes our past can keep us from sharing openly with our kids about sex. Is this the case for you? Do you carry baggage and condemnation from your sexual past? Friends, this is not from the heart of God. Romans 8:1 tells us "There is therefore now no condemnation for those who are in Christ Jesus." (ESV) Are you willing to lay that pain at the foot of the cross? Spend time asking God to take this baggage from you.

Day 2: Talking to your kids about sex should involve more than a discussion about physical purity. Ask the Lord to show you the struggles that your kids face with purity of mind and heart. Pray over these areas.

Day 3: Read Proverbs 22:6. You as parents have a unique opportunity to shape your children's view of their sexuality. You can pour in as much or as little as you want into this critical area of their lives. Ask God to help you map out here what steps you will take in the coming months to talk to your kids about the areas discussed in the DVD.

Day 4: If you could tell your children one thing about staying pure, what would it be? Why? Write it down here and pray about ways to communicate this principle to them.

• Remember that innocence does not equal ignorance.

Day 5: What did your parents tell you about sex? How would you have changed that? What did media tell you about sex? Was it accurate or truthful? Who was the most influential voice in your life when it came to sex?

session seven:
don't awaken love

[
"Patience is the companion of wisdom."
~St. Augustine
]

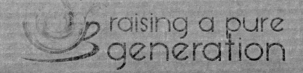
raising a pure
generation

don't awaken love

Come On In! Most young people are in search of the world's greatest love story. They want to be whisked off their feet into a fairy tale, Hollywood-style romance. But as parents, we know the reality of love, dating and marriage. We know the incredible journey that God Almighty is setting before them, and that God's love stories blow culture's out of the water! But how do we communicate our values about love and romance in a way that illuminates God's path and fades the glowing lights of Hollywood? Let's take a look at how to equip our kids to not awaken love until its time.

Song of Solomon 2:7

This is the season to fall deeply in love with the Lord

The four things that awaken love too soon

What they are and what we can do about them

- TV/Movies
- Books
- Music
- Friends

"Young women of Jerusalem, swear to me by the gazelles or by the does in the field that you will not awaken love or arouse love before its proper time."
Song of Solomon 2:7
(God's Word Translation)

NOTES

_____

_____

_____

_____

_____

_____

_____

_____

_____

_____

Preparing for their future spouses
Waiting instead of wasting time

Making your relationship something to strive for
Falling more deeply in love with the Lord yourself

 tech tip

Cell phones are like tiny computers. They have all of the benefits, and the downfalls, of our laptops. Cell phones make browsing online, uploading photos, and sending a text or email easy as cake. Unfortunately, the ease it creates for us adults can mean big problems for our young people. Accessing inappropriate content, sexting (sending nude pics), or having a virtual relationship has now become easier than ever. So how do you monitor that? Well, to keep up with what your kids are doing on their phones, we recommend these few tips:

1. Check your monthly bill. Know who your kids are talking to, when, and how often. If there is a number on the bill that you do not recognize, call it. KNOW who your kids are talking to.

2. Do not allow your tweens/teens to have cell phones with readily available internet access (like smartphones).

3. Do not put unlimited texting on your child's phone. This causes them to use their texts wisely, instead of constantly being on their phone.

 weekly challenge

As parents, come together and discuss the "awakening love" factor in your homes. Just as we've been discussing, awakening love too soon is often influenced by movies, TV, music, books and friends. Can you see how these mediums have influenced your kids? Take a look at the main categories again:

- **Movies/ TV:** What are your kids' favorite shows and movies? Are these helpful or harmful? Are there any in your home you need to get rid of?
- **Books:** Especially with romance novels and love stories, what are your kids' favorites? Do you know the content they are reading at home? At school?
- **Music:** Who are their favorite artists and what do they stand for? Are you familiar with their lyrics? Are they "romance" driven?
- **Friends:** Are your kids' friends boy/girl crazy? Are they keeping love asleep or determined to wake it up?

Now consider: What areas need to be adjusted in order to keep romantic love asleep in your children until the time is right?

 For more information and resources on keeping love asleep until its time, check out www.generationsofvirtue.org.

NOW AVAILABLE FOR TEENS:
CULTURE SHOCK PURITY CURRICULUM BY JULIE
HIRAMINE AND THE GENERATIONS OF VIRTUE TEAM!
DON'T MISS IT!

recommended resources

Birth-8 years

The Princess and the Kiss by Jennie Bishop
The Squire and the Scroll by Jennie Bishop
The Princess and the Three Knights by Karen Kingsbury
The Brave Young Knight by Karen Kingsbury
Knights, Maidens and Dragons by Julia Duin

8-12 years

Secret Keeper Girl Kits 1 & 2 by Dannah Gresh
His Mighty Warrior by Sheri Rose Shepherd
His Little Princess by Sheri Rose Shepherd

Teens

Culture Shock: Igniting a purity and integrity revolution by Julie Hiramine and the
   Generations of Virtue Team (11+)
When God Writes Your Love Story by Eric and Leslie Ludy
I Kissed Dating Goodbye by Joshua Harris (12+)
Hero: Becoming the man she desires by Fred Stoeker and Jasen Stoeker
Set-Apart Femininity by Leslie Ludy
How to Ruin Your Life by 40 by Steve Farrar

Parents

Choosing God's Best by Dr. Don Raunikar
Six Ways to Keep the "Little" in Your Girl by Dannah Gresh
Meet Mr. Smith by Eric and Leslie Ludy
Keeping Your Teen on the Road to Purity CD by Julie Hiramine
Age of Opportunity by Paul David Tripp

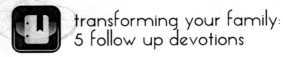

transforming your family:
5 follow up devotions

Day 1: Ponder Song of Solomon 2:7, which urges us "not to awaken love until the time is right." (NLT) How do you feel this applies to your own children? When do you feel the time is right?

- If the time our kids spend with us growing up prepares them for marriage, what are you doing right now to prepare them? What have you learned today about preparing your kids for marriage?

Day 2: For each of your children individually, what influences awaken love too soon in them? How can you come alongside them to disciple them through this? Ask the Lord to show you areas where love is being awakened in your family.

Day 3: Read 1 Timothy 4. It is normal for your kids to have crushes. As they get older, sometimes the crushes go from "That person is really cute" to "I really want to date that person!" Those are normal feelings that every parent deals with in their teens. Think through how you will handle the crushes your children have. How will you respond? Ask the Lord to show you how to help your children apply the instruction from 1 Timothy 5:2.

Day 4: Read Proverbs 11:2. As your children grow, they will deal with and process the various issues that all teens face. The question is not whether they will deal with "teen issues", but whether they will feel comfortable talking with you as they are walking through it. Today, think of and pray about three ways you can become a more approachable parent.

Day 5: Read Hebrews 13:4. Children in this day and age are hard-pressed to find examples of godly, loving relationships. Instead of passion, they see pain. Instead of intimacy, they see adultery. Are you modeling the kind of relationship that your child will look at and say, "I want to be married someday?" If there are issues in your marriage that are not positive, pray about these today. Pray for God to bring unity. Also pray for your child's future spouse.

session eight:

sacred love

["Give God the pen [to your love story].
The single reason He gave us the pen was
so that we could give it back to Him."
~Eric and Leslie Ludy]

raising a pure
generation

sacred love

Come On In! We all want our children to succeed in the area of relationships. But let's face it: The way culture tells us to go about things hasn't really worked out the last few decades. Despite the culture, though, we see young people all over the world who are striving for a different standard and committed to walking out pure relationships in God's timing. So what do these relationships look like, and how does it all work? Let's dive in to see what Sacred Love is all about.

The truth about dating and relationships
Make sure your expectations are clear

Emotional bonds
Keeping your heart, mind and body whole

20 second hug!

Why date, anyway?
Dating vs. waiting

TODAY'S MENU

SEXUAL PROMISCUITY *lifelong consequences*
Served with a side of emptiness and shame.
Pairs well with a broken heart.

HOMOSEXUALITY *inner turmoil*
Dished up with a heaping portion of turmoil.
Coupled with fear and dread.

PORNOGRAPHY *mental anguish*
Topped with devastation, wreckage, and ruin.
Add on a side of constant burden for no additional charge.

PURITY OF HEART *priceless*
Whipped up with a decadent portion of honesty
and integrity.

PURITY OF MIND *priceless*
Crowned with a generous slice of a clear conscience.
Couples perfectly with peace and love.

PURITY OF BODY *priceless*
Served atop a foundation of honor and respect.
Good reputation for no extra charge.

Definition of Yada

Definition of Shakab

"When the physical, emotional or spiritual level of involvement is greater than the commitment level, [you experience] counterfeit oneness... Dating emphasizes emotions, lust, and sensual desire—all of which demand a sexual response...Even singles who don't want to become physically involved often do because they are fighting the very natures God gave them."[1]

~From *Choosing God's Best* by Dr. Don Raunikar

NOTES

_____

_____

_____

_____

_____

1. The word study mentioned in the video referring to yada and shakab comes from *What Are You Waiting For?: The one thing no one ever tells you about sex* by Dannah Gresh. WaterBrook Press: 2011.

2. Raunikar, Don. *Choosing God's Best*, Multnomah Books: 1998. Pgs. 58-59

"Only about one in 50 kids for example had a sexually transmitted disease back in the 1960s. Today one in four of all adolescents has a sexually transmitted disease." (That means young people have a 1 in 4 chance of contracting an STD each year of high school)[3]

NOTES

_____

_____

_____

_____

_____

_____

_____

_____

Keys to a sacred love story
Building a relationship on the truth of God

3. McDowell, J. *The Bare Facts: 39 questions your parents hope you never ask about sex.* Chicago: Moody Publishers, 2011. Pg. 33

4. The information in the video about the 20 second hug comes from *Hooked: New science on how casual sex is affecting our children.* Joe S McIlhaney, Jr, MD and Freda Mckissic Bush, MD. Northfield Publising: 2008.

5. The statistics mentioned in the video about the ages of initial dating was taken from Josh McDowell and Dick Day's *Why Wait: What you need to know about the teen sexual crisis.* Thomas Nelson: 1994

REASONS TO DATE

TO FIND A MARRIAGE PARTNER

> • *Dating doesn't find you a marriage partner, God does*

LEARN HOW TO RELATE TO THE OPPOSITE SEX

> • *Dating doesn't teach you how to relate, it teaches you to have regrets*

DEVELOP SOCIAL SKILLS AND EMOTIONAL HEALTH

> • *Dating destroys emotional health*

TO HAVE FUN

> • *Dating replaces fun with resentment and hurt*

TO HAVE CERTAIN NEEDS MET UNTIL MY MARRIAGE PARTNER IS FOUND

> • *Only God can fill the void inside us and meet our needs*

The concepts for this chart came from *Choosing God's Best* by Dr. Don Raunikar. Multnomah Books: 1998.

recommended resources

Birth - 8 years
The Princess and the Kiss by Jennie Bishop
The Squire and the Scroll by Jennie Bishop
The Princess and the Three Knights by Karen Kingsbury
Knights, Maidens and Dragons by Julia Duin

8-12 years
Passport 2 Purity by Dennis and Barbara Rainey
Knights, Maidens and Dragons by Julia Duin

Teens
Culture Shock: Igniting a purity and integrity revolution by Julie Hiramine and the
    Generations of Virtue Team
God's Gift to Women by Eric Ludy
Answering the Guy Questions by Leslie Ludy
What Are You Waiting For?: The one thing no one ever tells you about sex
    by Dannah Gresh
Do Hard Things by Alex and Brett Harris
Passion and Purity by Elizabeth Elliott

Parents
Hooked by Dr. Joe S. McIlhaney Jr. and Dr. Freda McKissic Bush
Preparing Your Son for Every Man's Battle by Stephen Arterburn and Fred Stoeker
Preparing Your Daughter for Every Woman's Battle by Shannon Ethridge
Choosing God's Best by Dr. Don Raunikar
Moral Revolution: The naked truth about sexual purity by Kris Vallotton and
    Jason Vallotton
Have a New Teenager by Friday by Dr. Kevin Leman

tech tip

Kids are digital natives. We are the immigrants. So we can't assume that we "know our kids wouldn't do anything like that", because the reality is, when it comes to the internet, our kids could run circles around us. In order to keep track of where your kids are going, be sure you have the passwords for all of their social networking sites, music programs, chats, etc. Now, this isn't fool proof: your kids may have multiple social accounts under alias names, have music programs you've never heard of, or delete their chats if they don't want you to see. But having their passwords sets the standard that you do know what they are doing, and you are checking up on them.

ways to connect

For younger ones: Find one good example of a "God-written" love story and share it with your kids. This could be a movie, book, Bible story…anything you can find! Regularly share with them how awesome God's love stories are. For older ones: Define your version of a sacred love story. Sit down with your kids and establish the dating/relationship standard. What defines "ready to be in a relationship", etc. This activity will feed into the Weekly Challenge below.

weekly challenge

Relationships can be one of the stickiest subjects for any family, so it is important to have a plan, a sort of "course charted" when it comes to how you and your spouse are going to handle the million dollar question: To date or not to date? But how? you might ask. Well, try the ideas below to get you started. But whatever you do, remember to keep breathing, don't panic and know that God is on your side!

- Check out the resources available! Books like *Choosing God's Best* by Dr. Don Raunikar and Joshua Harris's *I Kissed Dating Goodbye* give a great perspective (these and many more are available at generationsofvirtue.org)
- Prayerfully establish your view on future relationships: Will you encourage dating? What age will they be allowed to pursue a relationship? What will the "requirements" be?
- Prayerfully establish your expectations for your children regarding their physical purity. And be specific. Do you expect them to be virgins on their wedding day? Do you expect your kids to refrain from sexual contact? Remember, there is a lot of ground to cover between handholding and having sex[6]. Where you do expect the line to be drawn?

By establishing your desire for your children's future relationships, you're helping them build godly convictions for a pure future.

 Don't forget: a great reminder for purity is purity rings and jewelry by Generations of Virtue. Browse our amazing selection at: generationsofvirtue.org

6. From *Passport 2 Purity* by Dennis and Barbara Rainey, FamilyLife Publishing: 2006.

transforming your family:
5 follow up devotions

Day 1: Read Galatians 5:1. Like we talked about in this session, bonding happens at a variety of levels. Can you see times in your own life when you have been bonded to someone of the opposite sex who was not your spouse? During this session, and during your prayer time now, are there any bonds from your past that the Lord wants to set you free from? Surrender what He brings to your mind back to Him completely.

Day 2: **It is said that children inherit** their view of relationships from their parents. How does that saying affect you? Was that true for your situation? Outside of marriage itself, what taught you the most about relationships? Oftentimes it is helpful to take a look at our own view so that we are able to see what we are passing onto our children. Go back and read Deuteronomy 6:1-9 and seek to pass on a godly heritage to the next generations.

Day 3: **Since you have gone through** the *Raising a Pure Generation* DVD Series, how has your view on dating and relationships evolved? In the future, what will your role be in your children's relationships? Write down 3 commitments in the arena of dating and relationships that God is impressing upon your heart.

- What is one of God's standards that you are already holding with your teens when it comes to relationships?

_____

_____

_____

_____

_____

_____

_____

_____

_____

_____

_____

_____

Day 4: Read Psalm 46. Teaching our kids "Yada" when the world is constantly throwing "Shakab" in their faces can be a pretty difficult thing to do. But as we grow deeper in our personal relationship with Jesus Christ, as we have "yada" with Him, our teaching then becomes by example. What areas in your walk with Christ is He prompting you to let go of the old and draw closer to have "yada" with Him?

- What's on the menu at your house? Is there a love for God created and an appetite for Him, or an appetite for things of the world?

Day 5: What is one thing the Lord taught you through this DVD series that you always want to remember? Write it down here. Now think of one thing you learned about love, purity, and relationships that you want to tell your children. (You could write your "one thing" to your children and mail it "snail mail" to them. Let it serve as a reminder for how your family is going to walk pure in heart, pure in mind and pure in body.)

A WORD ABOUT
GENERATIONS OF VIRTUE

The mission of Generations of Virtue is to equip parents, churches, schools and organizations to empower the next generation to be pure in our world today. Generations of Virtue isn't just a ministry - it's a movement to turn the tide of culture. Starting in 2003, GOV was founded by Julie Hiramine out of a realization that parents are facing a world that is intent on trampling their children's purity of heart, mind and body. Parents need to be prepared to train their kids to stand against this force from the enemy as they answer God's call on their lives. The questions are everywhere:

- How do we live lives of purity and integrity?
- How do I talk to my kids about sex?
- How do we equip our children to choose purity instead of the cheap imitation that this world has to offer?
- How can this generation see the Living God and His incredible plan for their lives?

Generations of Virtue is passionate about providing the latest, cutting-edge resources, dynamic teaching sessions and engaging tools that groups, churches, parents, teens and families can use to stand pure before God in heart, mind and body.

For upcoming events, practical resources, and to join the movement of raising up a holy generation, visit our website: www.generationsofvirtue.org

Visit Us Online!

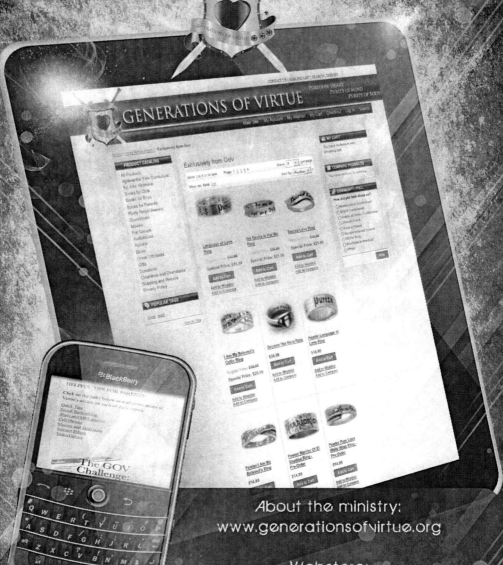

About the ministry:
www.generationsofvirtue.org

Webstore:
www.generationsofvirtue.org/store

Blogs:
For parents: generationsofvirtue.org/blog
For teens: apuregeneration.com

ANOTHER STUDY FROM JULIE AND THE GOV TEAM

★ CULTURE SHOCK

IGNITING AN INTEGRITY AND PURITY REVOLUTION

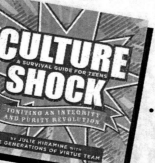

Culture Shock is an interactive, 5-session study for teens and leaders. Equip your teens to:

• See and learn how to refute the lies the enemy has told them about who they are and why they are here

• Use technology to advance God's Kingdom instead of fulfill selfish pursuits

• Surrender the popularity game and pursue true friendship with their peers

• Gain a new vision of God's design for romance, relationships, and love

• Answer God's awesome call on their lives!

Leader's Guide and Student's Guide available

Group quantity discounts available on our website:
www.generationsofvirtue.org/cultureshock

PURITY RINGS

AN OUTWARD SYMBOL OF AN INNER COMMITMENT

Our exclusive rings are available in
pewter and sterling silver.
Visit www.generationsofvirtue.org/store
to see all our styles.
GROUP DISCOUNTS AVAILABLE

AGAINST THE TIDE

In today's world, purity training needs to start young. *Against the Tide* makes it easy for parents to engage their children in conversations about sex education, character building, and relationships using the best resources on the market. This year-by-year guide gives parents a game plan to go through our top recommended resources, along with follow up discussion questions, tips and pointers we've found from using these resources ourselves.

Versions available:
Against the Tide Preschool-4th Grade
Against the Tide 5th-8th Grade

CPSIA information can be obtained at www.ICGtesting.com
Printed in the USA
LVOW12s0031210114

370140LV00005B/10/P